Coulda Woulda Shoulda

Baseball stories you haven't heard (yet)

C<small>HRIS</small> W<small>ILLIAMS</small>

Coulda Woulda Shoulda
Baseball Stories You Haven't Heard (Yet)

by Chris Williams

Edited by Gregory F. Augustine Pierce
Cover by Tom A. Wright
Cover photo of Kris Bryant and Anthony Rizzo:
    Jerry Lai—USA TODAY Sports, used with permission
Text design and typesetting by Courter & Company

Published by ACTA Sports, 4848 N. Clark Street, Chicago, IL 60640,
(800) 397-2282, www.actasports.com

Library of Congress Catalog number: 2017932799
ISBN: 978-0-87946-586-5
Printed in the United States of America by Total Printing Systems
Year 25 24 23 22 21 20 19 18 17
Printing 15 14 13 12 11 10 9 8 7 6 5 4 3 2 First

Contents

For the North Court Lane Gang:
Brian, Tim, Lee, Jerry, Bobby, and Mike.

"Thanks for your friendship and the memories!"

Introduction

———

Do you abhor baseball clichés? ("There's no such thing as a clutch hitter or pitcher!" "Defense wins titles." "The best teams only win 60% of the time.") So do I. I like pointing out they are not always true. But do you enjoy reading a good yarn about baseball's past? And do you like a few well-chosen stats sprinkled in without making the book seem like an insurance adjustors' manual?

Then you are in luck, because between the covers of this volume are a collection of twelve of my own (mostly) cliché-free essays that range, time-wise, from the very early years of the 1900s to the end of the 2016 World Series. Topics covered include the mystery of a Cubs team stocked with All-Stars and future Hall of Famers that finished in dead last, why a Yankees club fell into the second division after winning a pennant, how a White Sox team of hitless wonders won the World Series, and the unusual cases of a rookie who hit .313 in his rookie season only to be back permanently in the minors the following year and the first (and probably last) "designated runner" in the major leagues.

There is plenty of statistical analysis too, like why the 2016 World Series might have gone seven games—not because of any real or imagined curses but because the two teams were so evenly matched when the series began; how the Mets became truly amazing; why the Cincinnati Reds didn't need the mob to beat the Chicago "Black Sox"; and why Dick Allen belongs in the Hall of Fame.

There is also has a bit of human interest stuff, too, including the opening piece saluting the close friendship between Kris Bryant and Anthony Rizzo of the 2016 World Champion Chicago Cubs and comparing it (both positively and negatively) to the relationship between Babe Ruth and Lou Gehrig of the New York Yankees in the 1920s and 1930s. I share memories of my childhood trip to one of baseball's historic ballparks with my dad and end with a tongue-in-cheek satire on the years when baseball was really baseball.

I believe that life-busy fans who don't have the time or inclination to dig into the many outstanding, statistically-comprehensive books will appreciate the "detailed brevity" in these baseball stories I don't think you've heard yet (at least not as told by me). My hope is that this collection will trigger more than a few friendly debates between knowledgeable fans who either agree or disagree with my conclusions or engender the telling of new stories that I haven't heard (yet) either. It's those sort of conversations that make baseball such a fun sport for me to follow.

I also hope that younger baseball enthusiasts who read this book will gain an increased appreciation of a portion of the sport's remarkable past, and exciting present, and limitless future. To everyone who browses these pages, enjoy!

Chris Williams

YORK COUNTY, PA
Opening Day 2017

CHAPTER 1

Bookend Buddies

"I got you to look after me, and you got me to look after you, and that's why." — *John Steinbeck*

———

One of the great stories to come out of the exciting 2016 World Series centered on the close friendship that has developed between Cubs players Kris Bryant and Anthony Rizzo. It is totally appropriate that the final out of the Series, after a wait of 108 years, was a 6-3 double play, and the first baseman and third basemen on the play met at the pitcher's mound to start the celebration. (Rizzo later gave the ball to Tom Ricketts, the president and owner of the club.)

The Bryant-Rizzo relationship transcends the typical baseball season-long camaraderie to such a degree that the slugging pair are viewed as being inseparable. Because of this very public bond between the two men, teammates, fans, and the media often refer to the slugging pair as "Bryzzo."

This bromance (to use my first cliché of the book) between Rizzo and Bryant is very similar to the relationship that took place between baseball Hall of Famers Babe Ruth and Lou Gehrig, at least during the early years of their time together on the Yankees. As a young player, Gehrig idolized Ruth and the two would often be seen eating, playing cards, and traveling together. They barnstormed together in the offseason, along with sharing numerous golfing and fishing outings. From all appearances, the Yankee pair was extremely tight, much like the Cubs' Bryant and Rizzo appear to be today.

It is not an exaggeration to say that the four also share many similarities as ball players. Ruth and Gehrig were the center of a potent Yankees attack that won four pennants (1926, 1927, 1928, 1932) and three World Series (1927, 1928, 1932) during the nine years the two were teammates. Chicago's Bryant and Rizzo were the offensive hub of the 2016 NL pennant-winning and eventual World Championship team. Both Cubs are young (ages 24 and 27 at this writing) and have the talent to potentially spearhead their team to Yankee-like dominance in the coming years.

—

The first World Series that witnessed Ruth and Gehrig in the same lineup was in 1926 when the Bronx Bombers faced-off with the St. Louis Cardinals. It was a Series very similar to the 2016 match-up between the Cubs and Indians in that it went the full seven games. And as in 2016, when the Cubs were heavy favorites to win, the Yankees were expected to vanquish the Redbirds easily.

As often happens, the experts got it wrong. A scrappy Cardinals squad upset the powerful Yankees by taking the Series 4-3. The 31-year-old Ruth and the 23-year-old Gehrig performed fairly well during the seven games that were played. Ruth logged a .300 avg, banged out five homeruns, and drove-in five. Gehrig hit for a higher average (.348) but wasn't nearly as productive as he failed to plate anyone and managed only two extra base hits, both doubles. The Babe's production was somewhat marred by his failed steal attempt with two outs in the ninth inning of game seven. The Yanks were only down a run at the time, and many fans blamed Ruth for the Yankees failure that October.

Of course the Bryzzo-led 2015 Cubs, after vanquishing their archrival Cardinals, had failed miserably against the Mets in the NL Championship Series. It was a happier story in 2016, obviously. Led by Ben Zobrist and others (not only Bryant and Rizzo), the young Chicago team clawed their way back from a 3-1 games deficit to defeat a good Cleveland Indians squad in seven. It was just the sixth time in history that a team won the World Series after getting in a 3-1 hole. The only other years that kind of remarkable comeback took place were 1925 (Pirates over Senators), 1958 (Yankees over Braves), 1968 (Tigers over Cardinals), 1979 (Pirates over Orioles), and 1985 (Royals over Cardinals).

Zobrist captured the Series MVP award, thanks in large part to his sizzling .357 average and inspired play. Second year man Kris Bryant (who went on to win the 2016 NL MVP award) competed well under the pressure that goes along with playing in the Fall Classic. Number 17 slammed two key homeruns, drew five walks and logged a lofty .500 slugging percentage. His buddy and mentor, Anthony Rizzo, Number 44) contributed heavily with a .360 average that included a homerun, doubles, and five runs batted-in. In the locker room after game seven, Zobrist stated his opinion about Bryant and Rizzo's importance to the Cubs, "They're the heart of this team," the MVP said simply.

It's hard to argue with Zobrist's opinion. Over two campaigns (the first one starting about a month late because of contractual considerations), Bryant has averaged 34 homeruns and 106 runs-batted-in per season. Over six seasons, not all with the Cubs, Rizzo has averaged 29 homeruns and 92 runs-batted-in. The young pair are also a good influence in the Cubs' clubhouse, serious when appropriate but more than able to keep their teammates loose with their sense of humor. Without these two guys on the team, it's difficult to imagine the Cubs attaining the heights to which they have already achieved much less what I predict they will still accomplish.

—

Likewise, we can't conceive of the Yankees during the early Ruth-Gehrig years achieving the level of success they did without "The Bambino" and "The Iron Horse" in the middle of their lineup.

During his illustrious career, Ruth averaged 46 homeruns and 143 runs-batted-in per season. Gehrig also posted impressive numbers during his time in Yankee pinstripes, averaging 37 long balls and 149 runs plated.

Ruth and Gehrig's personal relationship wasn't as successful as their exploits at the plate. After several years of relative bliss, things began to sour. Gehrig was a disciplined, driven man, and Ruth's often-undisciplined lifestyle began to grate on the stoic first baseman's nerves. Gehrig kept quiet about his feelings, and their friendship might have survived this personality difference. But when Gehrig's mother publicly criticized Ruth's adopted daughter's clothing, the Babe went off on his teammate. "Don't ever speak to me again off the ball field!" Ruth barked at his one-time pal.

Gehrig was very close to his mother and highly protective of her. In addition, the Yankee first baseman had become a little suspicious about the relationship between his wife Eleanor and Ruth. This jealousy, together with a growing disgust with Ruth's lifestyle and anger about his teammate's criticism of his mother, fueled a deep-seated resentment in the Iron Horse. Soon, Gehrig was nursing a strong dislike of Ruth, a loathing that would last for years.

Thus, one of baseball's most-famous feuds was born. There are photos of the pair during this chilly period smiling as if everything was right with the world. Don't be fooled. It was all for show. Ruth and Gehrig had grown to detest each other.

Their quarrel came to an end—sort of—in 1939 at the famous "Lou Gehrig Appreciation Day" ceremony. Gehrig was dying of ALS (later dubbed "the Lou Gehrig disease") and had just given his touching "luckiest man alive" speech to the overflow crowd at Yankee Stadium. Ruth, always an emotional guy with a big heart, was deeply touched and took the opportunity to give Gehrig a big hug. A photo of the meeting shows a smiling Lou but strangely with no arm around the burly Ruth. It appears that Gehrig may not have completely forgiven his teammate.

—

I hope that Kris Bryant and Anthony Rizzo's relationship never goes the way of the two Yankee greats, but the pressure from the media on sports figures today is exponentially more intense than it ever was on Ruth and Gehrig. There is so much negativity in the world these days that I am really pulling for these two Cubs; their friendship is uplifting and encouraging to many fans, not just in Chicago, who are starved for some genuine good vibes.

Long live "Bryzzo!"

CHAPTER 2

Curse or No Curse

*"It is the mark of a truly intelligent person to be moved
by statistics." – George Bernard Shaw*

———

The 1919 World Series is marked one of the darkest sagas in baseball history. (That infamous early twentieth-century "fix"—universally known as the "Black Sox scandal"—is covered in more detail later in this book.) But did you ever think how unfair it was to the team that won? Can you even name them? When discussing what transpired that dark October, it's usually taken for granted that the Chicago White Sox were vastly superior to their World Series opponents, the Cincinnati Reds. Few gave Cincinnati much of a chance to vanquish a highly-touted Chicago club, but they did, albeit under the cloud of crookedness. However, a study of the stats shows that Cincy had a fine team that year and very well could have taken the 1919 Fall Classic without the help of several dishonest Sox players.

Now fast forward to 2016 and the showdown between the Chicago Cubs and the Cleveland Indians. Just like 1919, many weren't looking at the match-up as a showdown between two good teams. More like a smack down by the Cubs over the Tribe. And much of the pre-Series hype had to do with a "curse" or, if you will, a series of "curses" that had supposedly been cast on the Cubs many years before.

Back in 1945, miffed at Cub management banning his goat (yes, he did bring a goat to the ball park) from attending the World Series, tavern owner William Sianis allegedly pronounced that the Northsiders "ain't gonna win no more." It wasn't clear whether Sianis' curse meant that the Cubbies would never win another National League pennant—or another World Series—for dissing his bewhiskered pet. The Cubs went on to lose to the Detroit Tigers in the World Series that year, and in the subsequent 71 years managed to stumble in their efforts to secure the National League pennant in 1969, 1984, 1989, 1993, 2003, 2007, 2008, and 2015—all seasons in which they came close-but-no-cigar.

More than a few normally level-headed Cubs fans believed the curse of the goat might actually have something to do with the club's championship drought. Even many of those not given to superstition found Chicago's string of failures inexplicable. Then in 2003, when the Cubs were only four outs away from winning the National League pennant and go to the World Series, nice-guy Cubs fan Steve Bartman did what every fan in the world would do and tried to catch a foul ball in the left-field stands. The Cubs shortstop then booted a double-play ball, the Cubs lost that game and the one the next day to the Florida Marlins (who, by the way, went on to beat the Yankees in the World Series), and the "curse" was "confirmed."

(For real aficionados of Wrigley Field, there is a sign on one of the rooftops beyond the right field bleachers and across Sheffield Avenue that lists the number of years since the Cubs have won a division title, a league championship, and the World Series. A few years ago they had to add an extra digit on the third number to allow it to go over 100! During the 1916 season, the number read: 01-71-108. It now reads, as of this writing before the 2017 season begins: 00-00-000. Perhaps the sweetest number in Chicago Cubs history!)

The Wrigley faithful's hopes were buoyed during the 2016 season when their Cubbies roared through the regular season with 108 wins and then defeated both of their west-coast nemeses San Francisco Giants and Los Angeles Dodgers to win their first NL pennant in over seven decades. Perhaps the Sianis' curse really was over, but fans wouldn't know for sure until the final out of the World Series.

The Cubs' American League opponent would be the surprising Cleveland Indians, whom no one had expected to win much of anything. They were, of course, a solid team, but the vast majority of experts were certain that Chicago would have little or no problem winning the team's first World Series since 1908. With a powerful attack that scored 808 runs and crashed 199 homeruns during the regular season and a pitching staff that led the NL in era (3.15) and least hits allowed (1125 in 1460 innings), the Cubs looked like a sure-thing to beat the Indians—at least in the eyes of hungry Cubs fans. The "betting boys" in Las Vegas told them that Chicago was almost a 2-1 favorite to win it all. But Cleveland had other ideas. After all, it had been 74 years since they themselves had won a World Series! Unfazed by the hype and confident in their own abilities, they took heavily-favored Chicago to the seven game limit.

Talks of the curse had become rampant again after the Cubs lost three of the first four games of the series. At times they looked tight and appeared on the verge of coughing up the title once again. But they kept their collective cool, even after blowing a three-run lead in game seven, to complete a sweep of the last three games—all of them elimination contests for the Cubs—to stuff that curse up a certain aegagrus hircus' posterior.

—

Should the close contest in the 2016 World Series, which went through the tenth inning of the seventh game, have come as a great surprise? I think not. Those of us who had no dog in the fight and had studied the statistical matchups on both sides of the field knew (or should have known) better. Let me explain. What follows is a comparison and analysis of the 2016 Cubs and Indians starting lineups before the World Series began, based on their regular season stats, which were available to any sports fan with access to the Internet. (NOTE: I am comparing the players who actually ended up playing the positions they did in the series, although there were some surprises on both sides at several positions, including left field, center field, second base, DH, and catcher.)

First Base

Rizzo, Cubs .292 avg, 32 hr, 109 rbi, .385 obp
Napoli, Indians .239 avg, 34 hr, 101 rbi, .335 obp
Edge: Cubs

Comments prior to start of play: Napoli was a bit of a force himself with 34 dingers.

Second Base

Zobrist, Cubs .272 avg, 18 hr, 76 rbi, .386 obp, 6 sb
Baez, Cubs .273 avg, 14 hr, 59 rbi, .314 obp, 12 sb
Kipnis, Indians .275 avg, 23 hr., 82 rbi, .343 obp., 15 sb
Edge: Tie

Comments prior to start of play: Zobrist is one of my all-time favorite players, he and his perennial high obp; but Kipnis also had a good year at the plate. Zobrist and Baez were both solid offensively and their batting averages were nearly identical. As far as glove work is concerned, the fielding percentages for the guys who played the most were very close (Zobrist .984, Kipnis .981.) Baez was a decent second baseman with a .973 percentage, but he made spectacular plays. (Post-series comment: Zobrist ended up not playing an inning at second base in the series as young Baez won the spot by his MVP-level play in the first two rounds of the playoffs. This almost certainly would have given the pre-series edge to the Indians prior to the games.)

Shortstop

Russell, Cubs .238 avg, 21 hr, 95 rbi, .321 obp, 5 sb
Lindor, Indians .301 avg, 15 hr, 78 rbi, .358 obp, 19 sb
Edge: Indians

Comments prior to start of play: Lindor's average and obp were significantly higher than Russell's, plus the Indians' shortstop stole 19 bases to Russell's five. Russell did hit a few more homers and drove in a ton of clutch runs during the year, but Lindor fielded his position better with a .982 percentage to Russell's .975.

Third Base

Bryant, Cubs .292 avg, 39 hr, 102 rbi, .385 obp, 8 sb
Ramirez, Indians .312 avg, 11 hr, 76 rbi, .363 obp, 22 sb
Edge: Cubs

Comments prior to start of play: This edge may seem obvious. Bryant hit 28 more homeruns, drove in 26 more runs, and had a 25 point advantage in obp, but Ramirez was a better fielder (.979 to .966), had a higher batting average (.312 to .292), and stole 14 more bases (22 to 8). Ramirez was good enough during the year that you could easily argue that there was not as big an advantage to the Cubs at the hot corner. As a matter of fact, a case could be made that there was none. Both are fine, productive offensive players who don't kill their teams with shoddy glove work.

Left Field

Zobrist, Cubs .272 avg, 18 hr, 76 rbi, .386 obp, 6 sb
Davis, Indians .249 avg, 12 hr, 48 rbi, .306 obp, 43 sb
Edge: Cubs

Comments prior to start of play: Zobrist hit for a higher average, plated more runs, registered a higher obp. His fielding percentage was lower (.980 to .986) but he did register nine outfield assists to Davis' one. If Zobrist had started at second base, there were multiple ways the Cubs could have gone in left that would still have given them the edge, but Zobrist in left and Baez at second was always the most likely scenario, in my opinion.

Center Field

Fowler, Cubs .276 avg, 13 hr, 48 rbi, .393 obp

Naquin, Indians .296 avg, 14 hr, 43 rbi, .372 obp
Edge: Slightly to Indians

Comments prior to start of play: Fowler did have a higher obp and rbi total. But along with a higher batting average, Naquin compiled a better slugging percentage (.514 to .447) and fielding average (.990 to .983). Both men have strong arms and racked-up six assists each.

Right Field
Heyward, Cubs .230 avg, 7 hr, 49 rbi, .325 obp
Chisenhall, Indians .286 avg, 8 hr, 57 rbi, .328 obp
Edge-Indians

Comments prior to start of play: Chisenhall topped Heyward offensively. Heyward was a better fielder (.993 to .986) and—it turned out—a better motivational speaker!

Catcher
Montero, Cubs .216 avg, 8 hr, 33 rbi, .327 obp
Ross, Cubs .229 avg, 10 hr, 32 rbi, .338 obp
Contreras, Cubs .282 avg, 12 hr, 35 rbi, .357 obp
Ferdorwicz, Cubs .194 avg, 0 hr, .212 obp
Gomes, Indians .167 avg, 9 hr, 34 rbi, .201 obp
Perez, Indians .183 avg, 3 hr, 17 rbi, .285 obp
Gimenez, Indians .216, 4 hr, 11 rbi, .272 obp
Edge: Cubs

Comments prior to start of play: Chicago's catching corps were better with the stick even before utility man Contreras' solid contributions.

Are you starting to see a trend here? At no position (except perhaps at catcher) did the Cubs completely blow out the Indians, production-wise, before the Series began. Even at the positions where Chicago fielded a better player, the Indians had a guy who is pretty good himself, which is usually the case in any World Series.

—

Let's move on to the starting pitching. Remember, this is the conventional statistical analysis prior to the start of the playoffs, based on each pitcher's 2016 regular season stats.

#1 Guy

Lester, Cubs 19-5, 2.44 era, 197 K, 1.01 whip,
   0 shutouts
Kluber, Indians 18-9, 3.14 era, 227 k, 1.05 whip,
   2 shutouts
Edge: Tie

Comments prior to start of play: This is a tough one. My first inclination was to give Lester the edge with the lower era and whip, but Kluber's era wasn't bad, his whip was very good, he struck out 30 more batters, and hurled a couple of shutouts. No clear winner here.

#2 Guy
Arietta, Cubs 18-8, 3.10 era, 197 K, 1.08 whip
Bauer, Indians 12-8, 4.26 era, 168 K, 1.31 whip
Edge: Cubs

Comments prior to start of play: Just look at the stats.

#3 Guy
Hendricks, Cubs 16-8, 2.13 era, 170 K, 0.97 whip
Tomlin, Indians 13-9 4.40 era, 118 K, 1.19 whip
Edge: Cubs

Comments prior to start of play: Again, stats don't lie.

#4 Guys
Lackey, Cubs 11-8, 3.35 era, 180 K, 1.05 whip
Hammel, Cubs 15-10, 3.83 era, 144 K, 1.20 whip
Carrasco, Indians 11-8 3.32 era, 150 K, 1.14 whip
Salazar, Indians 11-6, 3.87 era, 161 K, 1.34 whip
Edge: Tie

Comments prior to start of play: Four decent pitchers who made significant contributions in 2016.

Okay. Chicago had better starting pitchers, and the fact that they compiled a staff era of 3.15, playing half of their games in often (but not-so-much-in-2016) offense-friendly Wrigley Field is impressive. But the Tribe's first four weren't chopped liver, and in a seven-game series staff ace Kluber would most likely start three games. Using your ace in such a fashion can mask certain pitching weaknesses evident during a 162-game regular season.

Next, we examine the bullpens, again using 2016 regular season stats prior to the start of the playoffs.

Closers

Chapman, Cubs 1-1, 1.01 era, .825 whip, 16 saves, 13.0 K per nine innings pitched

Allen, Indians 3-5, 2.51 era, 1.00 whip, 32 saves, 11.5 K per nine innings pitched

Edge: Cubs

Comments prior to start of play: Chapman with his miniscule 1.01 era and microscopic .825 whip. In addition, his strikeout ratio per nine innings was better. But Allen is very good, one of the best, and there is always the question of Chapman's emotional state of mind.

Bullpens

Edge: Indians

Comments prior to start of play: Cleveland's three top set-up men (Miller, Shaw, and Otero) performed significantly better during the season than their World Series counterparts (Rondon, Strube, Montgomery). Miller especially dominated during the AL playoffs.

Bench

Edge: Cubs

Comments prior to start of play: The edge here clearly belongs to the Cubs. With overall higher batting averages and more long balls, this pre-series match-up went to Chicago, and that was before Kyle Schwarber (16 hr in 2015) got cleared for DH and pinch-hitting duty at the last minute.

Managers

Edge: Tie

Comments prior to start of play: Both Joe Maddon and Terry Francona are proven winners and among the best in baseball.

—

Statistically, even before a pitch was made in the World Series of 2016, it was obvious to me that the 2016 Chicago Cubs were a better team than the 2016 Cleveland Indians, especially after Cleveland lost two of its top three starters during the regular season, but it was also clearly not the slam dunk (to mix sports metaphors) people might have thought before the series began, nor is it obvious now. The Cubs deserve tons of credit for hanging tough and not folding after getting down 3-1. They are a very talented club and barring major injuries should be a powerhouse for the foreseeable future.

BUT. (There's that word again.) It's also evident to me that the Indians had a pretty darn good club that deserved to be on the field and almost pulled off a "surprise" (not to them and not to me) victory. They weren't "lucky" or some sort of "Cinderella" club that almost managed to steal the World Series from a vastly superior team. If they had ultimately prevailed, it shouldn't have come as a great surprise. And it wouldn't have been because of some "curse" that some tavern owner proclaimed in 1945.

In fact, look at a couple of things that actually happened in the series. First of all, in left field (where the Cubs had arguably their biggest matchup advantage and where Ben Zobrist actually did win the World Series MVP Award), it was his counterpart Rajai Davis who tied game seven in the bottom of the eighth with a two-run homerun off the great Cubs closer, Aroldous Chapman, and set every Cubs fan in the world (including Zobrist) looking over their shoulder for a goat. And while Chapman did prove to be a great closer throughout the playoffs, it was a 25-year-old rookie, Carl Edwards, Jr., and a recent acquisition from the Seattle Mariners, former starter Mike Montgomery, who actually got the final three outs, thereby ending—if you insist—the "curse."

So, just like 1919, when the Reds "upset" the White Sox (albeit with a little help from the mob) and got no credit for doing so, it was right there in the stats for the Cleveland Indians to have a good chance to win the World Series in 2016. They just didn't. But don't say they couldn't have or didn't deserve to.

CHAPTER 3

From The Penthouse to the Outhouse

"The mighty warriors—fallen, fallen—in the middle of the fight!" – 1 Samuel 1:25

———

How does a team go from winning 99 games and the American League pennant one season to finishing eight games under .500 and way out of contention the next? When the proud New York Yankees franchise did just that in 1965, many fans couldn't believe it. How could a club with household-name position players like Mickey Mantle, Roger Maris, Elston Howard, Tony Kubek, Clete Boyer, and Bobby Richardson, and pitchers like Whitey Ford, Jim Bouton, Al Downing, Pedro Ramos, and a young Mel Stottlemyre on the roster collapse so far, so fast? Here's how.

—

The pitching staff wasn't to blame. Here are some two-year stats for the front four of their 1965 rotation:

	1964	1965
Whitey Ford	17-6, 2.13 era	16-13, 3.24 era
Jim Bouton	18-13, 3.02 era	4-15, 4.82 era
Al Downing	13-8, 3.47 era	12-14, 3.40 era
Mel Stottlemyre	N/A	20-9, 2.92 era

Jim Bouton, later the author of the book *Ball Four*, battled an injury in 1965 that sharply limited his effectiveness. However, rookie Mel Stottlemyre more than picked up the slack with a 20-9 record and 2.63 era. Whitey Ford fell off a little, but he still won 16 games. With better offensive support, the lefty might have logged 20 victories.

The Bronx Bombers' bullpen wasn't bad in 1965 either. Closer Pedro Ramos compiled a 2.92 era with 19 saves in 92 innings of work. The year before, the team's closer was Pete Mikkelson. His 1964 stats included 12 saves to go along with a 3.56 era over 86 innings. As a set-up man in

1965, Mikkelson was even more effective (3.28 era in 41 games), and Steve Hamilton appeared in 46 games and posted a stellar 1.39 era. The overall team era in 1965 was a respectable 3.28, just .13 higher than 1964.

So, the team's slide in 1965 can't be laid at the feet of the pitching staff. They did a decent job and gave the Yankees plenty of opportunities to win.

—

What killed the Yankees in 1965 was their offense, in particular their inability to get on base early and often (my second cliché). Below are the season comparisons. Pay attention to the on-base percentage (obp) and keep in mind that a "good" obp is at least .340, and anything below .300 is a bad joke. (For example, in 2016 the Chicago Cubs' team obp was .343, while the last place San Diego Padres' team obp was .299.)

	1964	1965
Mickey Mantle	.303 avg, 35 hr .423 obp	.255 avg, 19 hr .379 obp
Elston Howard	.313avg, 15 hr .371 obp	233, 9 hr .278 obp
Bobby Richardson	.267 avg .294 obp	.247 avg .287 obp
Tony Kubek	.229 avg .275 obp	.218 avg .258 obp
Clete Boyer	.218 avg .269 obp	.251 avg .304 obp
Tom Tresh	246 avg, 16 hr .342 obp	.279 avg, 26 hr .348 obp
Roger Maris	.281 avg, 26 hr .364 obp	.239 avg, 8 hr .357 obp
Phil Linz	.250 avg .332 obp	.207 avg .281 obp
Hector Lopez	.260 avg, 10 hr .317 obp	.261 avg, 7 hr .322 obp
Joe Pepitone	.251 avg, 28 hr .281 obp	.247 avg, 18 hr .305 obp

Except for Tresh and Boyer, all of the Yankee's most-used position players had noticeable declines in offensive production in 1965. In 1964, the Yankees had a team on-base percentage of .317. Not a great number, but with Mantle, Maris, and Pepitone driving a lot of balls over the fence, they were scoring some runs. In 1965, the team obp fell 18 points to .299. Crippled by injuries to Mantle and Maris and an off-year by Pepitone, the long balls weren't as frequent as before. As a consequence, the Yankees scored 611 runs in 1965 compared to 730 in 1964. That is an average of almost a run a game. Hence the trip to the outhouse.

—

Another obvious problem for the Yanks in 1965 was their defense. The team wasn't making as many of the routine plays as they did when they won the pennant the year before. In 1964, the Yankees finished second in the league in fielding. In 1965, they fell to sixth as some of the opponents' rallies that had been snuffed out by a great piece of glove work (by Kubek or Richardson or Boyer or someone else) the year before, now got new life with a Yankee miscue.

But the main reason the 1965 Yankees fell so far, so fast was the disintegration of the core of their offensive attack (Mantle, Maris, and Pepit-one hit 44 fewer homers than the previous year) coupled with the fact that most of the supporting cast, many of whom never got on base that much even in good years, were unable to step up and compensate for the lack of fire power, dooming the club to mediocrity a year after being in the World Series.

The Yankee slide would not end in 1965. The club would bottom-out with a last place finish in the AL (tenth out of ten teams) in 1966. The first Yankee dynasty (29 pennants) ended with the 1965 collapse. The team would rebuild (of cour$e), and by the early 1970s the Yankee pin-stripers were once again considered one of base-ball's elite franchises. But for a time the House That Ruth Built resembled Fenway or Wrigley for futility.

CHAPTER 4

The Year the Mets Became Amazin'

*"When you're hot, you're hot. And when you're not,
you're not."* —Jerry Reed

———

Manager Casey Stengel thought his Mets were "amazin'" in the early years of the franchise. For most New Yorkers, a winning streak of two or three games by the team from Queens might have been good reason to launch a congressional investigation. The Mets were bad, but with a roster populated by eccentric characters such as "Marvelous" Marv Throneberry, Choo-Choo Coleman, Jimmy Piersall, and "Hot Rod" Kanehl many Mets fans came to love the team. The first batch of Mets teams put some of the fun back into what is still basically a kid's game played by grown men.

After finishing ninth (out of ten teams in the

NL) in 1968, the Mets shocked the baseball world by capturing the Eastern Division title, the National League pennant, and the World Series in 1969. What makes what happened even more "amazin'" is the fact that the Mets came from way behind to beat out an excellent Chicago Cubs team to do it.

—

On paper, the Cubbies were powerful. Their starting lineup included three future Hall of Famers (Ernie Banks, Billy Williams, and Ron Santo) and three other All-Stars (Don Kessinger, Randy Hundley, and Glen Beckert).

In 1969, Mr. Cub hit 23 homeruns and drove in 106, Williams drilled 33 dingers and compiled 95 rbi, Santo plated 123 runs while slugging 29 homers, shortstop Kessinger hit 38 doubles and scored 109 runs, and second baseman Beckert hit .291. Catcher Hundley added 18 round-trippers and 64 rbi to the mix.

Journeyman outfielder Jim Hickman, who had actually played for the Mets in their early days, contributed 21 homeruns to the Cubs' offensive barrage.

New York's attack was spearheaded by outfielder Cleon Jones, who had a career year in 1969 with a .340 average, 75 rbi, and 12 homeruns. Tommy Agee patrolled center and played well there and hit .271 with 76 rbi, and second baseman Ken Boswell added a steady glove to go along with a good .279 average. Catcher Jerry Grote was outstanding defensively and was no automatic out at the plate with a .252 batting average.

Both teams had good benches in 1969. The Cubs could call on seasoned veterans Paul Popovich (.312 avg), Al Spangler (23 rbi), and Willie Smith (9 homeruns in 223 plate appearances). For the Mets, Art Shamsky hit .300 and slugged 14 homeruns as a part-time player and Don Clendenon stroked 12 round-trippers. Infielder Al Weis didn't hit much, but he played short stop, second base, and third base as the key utility man for New York skipper Gil Hodges.

Defensively, neither team gave away a lot of games with shabby glove work. The Mets finished second in fielding with a .980 percentage; the Cubs were right behind at .979.

—

A comparison of the pitching staffs is less clear. The Mets' had a good starting rotation in 1969. Tom Seaver won 25 games while posting a 2.21 era, Jerry Kooseman added 17 wins to go with his 2.28 era, Gary Gentry was solid with 13 victories, and Don Cardwell and Jim McAndrew combined for 14 wins.

The Mets bullpen was good too. Ron Taylor won nine and saved 13, Tug McGraw saved 12 while winning nine, and young fire baller Nolan Ryan registered six victories while striking out 92 in 89 innings.

But the Cubs had some guys who could pitch, too. Future Hall of Famer Fergie Jenkins anchored a fine Cub rotation that included Bill Hands and Ken Holtzman. Jenkins finished 1969 with 21 wins, Hands won 20, and Holtzman registered 17 victories. Number four starter Dick Selma notched ten wins and a respectable 3.63 era.

In the bullpen, manager Leo Durocher had "The Vulture" Phil Regan (12 wins, 17 saves) and reliable veterans Ted Abernathy (3.16 era) and Hank Aguirre (2.60 era) at his disposal.

In retrospect, the Mets had a slight edge in pitching due mainly to the outstanding performance of staff ace Tom Seaver and the tandem of Taylor and McGraw in the bullpen. These two gave Hodges more quality innings down the stretch than manager Leo Durocher's "go-to" guys did for the Cubs.

—

The Cubs built a nine-game lead in the Eastern Division of the NL by the middle of August and looked like a lock to make the playoffs. The Mets were playing good ball but no one expected them to overtake the juggernaut Chicago team that played their home games at Wrigley Field. And remember, there were no wild cards back then. You either won your division (there were only two divisions—eastern and western—in both the NL and the AL at the time) or went home and cried in your beer (my third cliché).

—

But then a really amazing thing happened. New York got red-hot while Chicago cooled off like a head of iceberg lettuce. Over the last two months of the season, the Mets went 44-17 while the Cubs sputtered home with a 27-29 record. The Eastern Division title was lost in September when the Cubs went 8-17, including a season-long eight-game losing streak at the beginning of the month.

When the dust had settled on October 1, Chicago found themselves in second place in the East, nine games behind the team they had led by the same amount just seven weeks earlier! What happened? What would cause such a talented team to fold? Or such an unlikely new team to rise so dramatically?

—

One obvious reason why the Mets overtook and then crushed the Cubs is timing. Sometimes it does matter when you win your games. Sure, early season losses might haunt you later, but the Mets were only five games under .500 on May 27. They were not the first team to get hot late in the season and finish in first place; it's just that New York's past history of ineptness made their success so surprising. Had the Pirates or the Cardinals accomplished the same thing in 1969, it wouldn't have been so amazing.

The Cubs, meanwhile, lost a bunch of games they should have been winning. They forgot that the season doesn't end on Labor Day, and the Mets streaked by them like the tortoise did the hare.

The real reason for the Mets' 1969 success was that many of their guys played incredibly well over the last two months of the season. Players that were average fielders made spectacular plays in the field; .200 hitters got clutch hits when they should have been whiffing; and it seemed like the Mets' pitchers were getting all the borderline calls. The few homeruns the Mets hit seemed to go out of the park at just the right time, and the injury bug decided to boycott Shea Stadium throughout August and September. Everything bounced right for the Mets during that time. Couple that with the fact they had a young, improving team, the New Yorkers scaled the baseball summit in dramatic fashion.

I also think the Cubs simply got tired down the stretch. Chicago had an older squad; some people believe that veteran manager Durocher should have rested the regulars more when the team had their big lead earlier in the season. The Cubs' roster averaged 29.2 years of age with three guys (Banks, Williams, and Hickman) in the starting lineup over 30. (Compare that with the 2016 Cubs championship team where, with the exception of senior-citizen catcher David Ross, almost every key player was under 30 years old.) The front-end of Chicago's 1969 bullpen was populated by grizzled veterans, ages 38, 36, and 32 (Aquirre, Abernathy, and Regan).

The Mets were considerably younger than the Cubbies, with an average age of 25.8. The "oldsters" in their daily lineup (Jones, Grote, and Agee) averaged only about 26. Out in the bullpen, Taylor, McGraw, and Ryan were 31, 24, and 22 respectively. In their head-to-head games against each other in September, the youthful New Yorkers outscored the gang from the Windy City 112-78. Meanwhile, against other clubs, the New York pitching staff limited the opposition to 70 runs down the stretch, while tired Cub hurlers allowed 119 tallies.

Cubs skipper Durocher probably kept the pedal to the metal (my fourth cliché) in an effort to wrap things up early and be able to give his team a good rest before the playoffs. Didn't happen. According to analyst Bill James, this was a major, avoidable error in judgment: "Durocher was going through maybe his 25th pennant race. Durocher should have had the foresight to see where this was headed."

So it appears in hindsight that a tired Chicago Cubs team watched a good team with fresher legs overtake them to win the Eastern Division title. Had "Leo the Lip" rested some of his players a little in May, June, and July, the outcome may have been different. Sure, the Mets might have still bested the Chicagoans, but it's doubtful that they would have left their rivals in the dust.

—

For the Mets, the magic continued. They knocked-off the Braves in the playoffs and shocked another talented squad, the Baltimore Orioles by winning the World Series four games to one. As Jerry Reed once sang, "When You're Hot, You're Hot." For two and a half months in 1969, the New York Mets were definitely hot. As hot, I believe, as any team has ever been. They were simply amazin'.

And the Cubs, well, they simply had to wait another 48 years to get it done. When you're not, you're not.

CHAPTER 5

My First
Baseball Thrill

*"There is something special about baseball that goes far
deeper than being a game. It is the father-son relationship
that is built, the life lessons that are taught in the process
of playing a game, and the ability to overcome not
succeeding all of the time and still considering yourself
a success." – John A. Passaro*

One of the biggest thrills of my life was the time
my father took me to see the Phillies and the
Dodgers play a doubleheader in Philadelphia on
September 15, 1967. Dad worked a lot of hours
and I didn't get much one-on-one time with him,
so the chance to hang out with him for several
hours at old Connie Mack Stadium was very
cool.

I was ten-years-old and already a die-hard
Phillies fan. My favorite player was Richie Allen

and I was plenty disappointed that Number 15 was on the DL and wouldn't be able to play that night. But besides that, the evening was magical.

For starters, Dad had secured box seats behind home plate, allowing us to see the action close-up. I had been to the ballpark at Twenty-first and Lehigh before, but we always saw the games from some distant, upper-deck, much cheaper perch. The panoramic view of the inside of the stadium from those box seats that night was breathtaking to a young kid: The high arc lights bathed the plush green grass carpet with a simple glory that gave the playing field a cathedral-like aura.

The massive scoreboard in right field towered like a giant that taunted left-handed hitters to just try and hit one over it. The encroaching darkness of night cast eerie shadows on the near-empty red and brown left-field bleachers. Just beyond the centerfield wall, the Stars and Stripes flapped vigorously on an ancient pole.

—

"Kinda windy," I said.

Dad nodded. "There's a hurricane out in the Atlantic."

This news concerned me. Would the storm interrupt the doubleheader?

"Don't worry, Chris. Doria is no threat to the Philadelphia area."

"Doria? Who's that?"

"That's the name of the hurricane."

"Oh," I said as a hot dog wrapper swirled past us. I felt very relieved.

Dad looked out at the flagpole. "The wind's blowing in," he said. "It's going to be a factor in these games."

And he was right.

—

Game number one featured a pitching match-up between Jim Bunning of the Phillies and Bill Singer of the Dodgers. Singer was having a good year, but Bunning was one of the league's premier hurlers and I expected the Phils to triumph. Number 14 pitched well-enough to win, allowing just four hits over eight innings, but Singer was just a bit better. Dodger catcher John Roseboro punctured the wind with a solo homerun in the top of the fourth, and Los Angeles won 1-0.

I tried to look on the bright side. "At least

Gonzalez got two hits," I told my father following the last out. Tony Gonzalez played left field for the Phillies and was in a battle for the 1967 batting championship with Pittsburgh's Roberto Clemente.

Dad nodded tolerantly. He was never a fan of statistics that didn't lead directly to victories. "Drysdale's pitching the second game," he said, almost ominously.

I interpreted Dad's words as a strong inference that he thought the Phillies had a good chance of getting swept that night. "But we got Chris Short!" I bristled. I knew Don Drysdale was great, but lefty Short was pretty darn good, too.

"Short's had some arm problems this year," Dad reminded me as the stadium ground crew worked on getting the field ready for the night-cap. He had grown up in Maine and was a Red Sox fan. He wasn't trying to provoke me; he just trying to be honest.

"Drysdale hasn't been so hot this year," I argued. Going into the game, the Dodger righty had a record of 10-15.

Dad smiled. "I guess we'll see, won't we?" he said.

—

Both pitchers went the distance in game number two. The wind continued to be a factor as Dad and I and the other 12,016 in attendance witnessed another 1-0 ball game. Chris Short held the Dodgers to seven hits and struck out six; Don Drysdale limited my team to six hits and fanned five.

Late in the game, Tony Gonzalez brought the Philly crowd to their feet when he launched a high fly ball to left field, a shot that appeared to be gone off the bat. But wind gusts roaring in towards home plate knocked the ball down, allowing Dodger left fielder Lou Johnson to make the catch on the warning track.

Los Angeles finally broke through when Wes Parker drove in the winning tally in the ninth inning.

For the first time since 1955, the Phillies had been shut out in both games of a doubleheader. Dad and I didn't get up to leave right away. Even though my team had been swept, I didn't feel empty. I lovingly scanned the inside of the stadium a few more times. My father seemed to understand and waited.

"Too bad we couldn't see them win at least one," Dad said when we finally headed for the exits.

"That's okay," I told him. "I had a great time."

He smiled and gently squeezed my arm.

One thing I didn't do at the time was thank him. Dumb kid. Thanks, Dad. I will cherish memories of September 15, 1967, for the rest of my life.

CHAPTER 6

Should Dick Allen Be in the Hall of Fame?

"It is hard to imagine a more polarizing figure in Philadelphia sports history than Dick Allen."
— Mitchel Nathanson

It is not really arguable that Dick Allen was one of the greatest players to ever wear a Philadelphia Phillies uniform. He also starred for three other teams during his 15-year career. Some fans believe that Allen wasn't just an outstanding Phillie; they feel he was one of the greatest players in major league baseball history. Many have campaigned to have Allen inducted into the Hall of Fame; his inclusion on the Hall's "Golden Committee" ballot in 2014 buoyed hopes that Allen might finally get the recognition he deserves. But he fell one vote short (getting eleven of the twelve votes needed from the veterans committee to get in). He is eligible again in December of 2017.

Does Dick Allen belong in the Hall of Fame?

—

To begin, let's examine Allen's entire career. Baseball is a game where numbers have been faithfully and carefully accumulated for over 100 years, and therefore you can compare players from wildly different eras. Allen's stats are impressive, no matter how you count them or whose you compare them to. During his first full season (1964), he hit .318 with 29 homeruns and 91 rbi to earn National League Rookie-of-the-Year honors. Two seasons later, he tore apart opposition pitching with a .317 average that included 40 homeruns and 110 rbi. (His 1966 figures would have been even more impressive had he not missed 20 games due to an injury.)

But Allen was not just a run-of-the-mill power hitter. He was a force of nature. Hall of Fame pitcher Tom Seaver listed the man from Wampum, Pennsylvania, as the player who scared him the most. Allen didn't just hit homeruns; his round-trippers were often titanic blasts. During his first stint with the Phillies (1963-1969), the club played their home games at Connie Mack Stadium, which featured a two-deck grandstand in left field. Allen crushed balls that landed on and over the roof of these stands on several occasions.

In 1967, Allen hit a pitch thrown by Nelson Briles of the Cardinals at the old ball park that traveled an estimated 529 feet. The ball was last seen sailing past the flagpole in dead center field. A year later, Number 15 hit one that cleared the gigantic 75-foot-high scoreboard in right field.

—

Allen's offensive production continued through the late 1960s, but his relationship with many Philly fans (but not me) was terrible. The problem began in 1965 when he and veteran journeyman Frank J. Thomas (not The Big Hurt) were both on the Phillies and were involved a pregame altercation with racial overtones. This fight led to Thomas' release, resulting in fans booing Allen unmercifully whenever he came to bat or made a mistake in the field. Of course, the boos would be replaced by thunderous cheers whenever the slugger would launch another moonshot into the North Philadelphia night sky.

Allen had been forced to tolerate verbal taunts from hometown Philly fans, including racial epithets. Some fans took to throwing small items at him from the stands, such as batteries, bolts, and coins. To protect himself from thrown objects, Allen wore a batting helmet while playing the field. Hate mail addressed to him regularly arrived at Connie Mack Stadium.

In the face of near-constant abuse, Allen publicly expressed his desire to be traded. Club management demurred, not wanting to part company with their talented slugger. In frustration, Allen began to do things he felt would force the Phillies to deal him to another team. He showed-up late for games, occasionally arrived at the ballpark under the influence of alcohol, and missed team buses and planes. It was during this phase of his career that Allen gained a reputation as a troublemaking problem child.

Allen himself has admitted that he didn't always handle the adversity in the best manner. "At the time, I thought I was the victim of racism," he explained years later. "I was also something of a jerk. There were others who had to deal with racism, and some of them handled it better than I did."

To be fair, Allen was under a pressure that few have had to experience in any walk of life, not just baseball. Was it his responsibility to "just take it" from thousands of hometown fans who attended games at Connie Mack Stadium? Can he be faulted for trying to do something to improve his life and pursue his career? Would the morons who heaped abuse on this man stick around under similar circumstances or would they have looked for a way to escape?

The answers to these questions seem obvious.

—

Allen finally got his wish after the 1969 campaign when he was dealt to the Cardinals. After posting good stats for St. Louis in 1970 and the Dodgers in 1971, Allen found himself a member of the Chicago White Sox in the spring of 1972. There he enjoyed his best season since 1966. He hit .308 while walloping 37 homeruns and drove in 113 runs to go along with a .603 obp. Allen was never considered a great fielder, but in 1972 he finished second in the AL in first base fielding percentage. For his efforts, Dick Allen was named the American League MVP. It was a golden year and the high water mark of his career. Injuries limited Allen's playing time in 1973, but in 1974 he led the AL in homeruns (32) before announcing his retirement in September.

With the Phillies playing in Veterans Stadium, a newer, more modern ball park, and expected to be in contention, however, Allen was convinced to rejoin the team in 1975, but the layoff coupled with no spring training took its toll; Allen hit .233 with 12 long balls in 1975. He rebounded somewhat in 1976 and was hitting well over .300 at the All-Star break when an injury slowed him down in the second half and limited his playing time. In 85 games that year, Allen hit 15 homeruns and drove in 49. Had he maintained that level of production over the entire season, his final tally would have been close to 30 homers and over 90 rbi.

After the1976 season, the Phillies and Allen parted company again. The Oakland A's were looking for some pop in their lineup and signed the aging slugger for 1977. After appearing in 54 games, Allen decided to call it quits for good.

—

The question of whether Dick Allen deserves a spot in Cooperstown can be answered by comparing his career numbers with those who are already in the Hall. It would be easy to favorably compare Number 15's stats with those of, let's say, Rabbit Maranville or Bill Mazeroski. Offensively, neither of these outstanding players came close to doing what Allen did at the plate. But that would be too easy and a bit unfair. Rabbit and Bill were tremendous glove men who got their share of hits, and they were also vital members of some great teams. But neither of them put up the kind of numbers that Allen did. Conversely, Allen never approached their greatness as fielders.

An excellent comparison can be made, however, between Allen and Tony Perez. Elected to the Hall of Fame in 2000, Perez played 23 years in the major leagues. Like Allen, he spent most of his career at third and first. They both played during the same era, so statistical adjustments won't need to be made for factors like the dead ball, day-time baseball, seasonal league hitting and pitching norms, etc. Let's compare their overall career stats:

> Perez .279 avg, .341 obp, .463 slug, 379 hr,
>   1652 rbi, 1272 runs
> Allen .292 avg, .378 obp, .534 slug, 351 hr, 1119 rbi,
>   1099 runs

So, you can see that Dick Allen's 15-year career compares favorably with Perez's. It's true that Perez had more life-time homers, ribbies, and runs than Allen, but he played eight more seasons. What kind of numbers would the Wampum Walloper have compiled had his career lasted 23 years? Allen had a higher lifetime average and on-base percentage than Perez, and in eight less seasons hit just 28 less homeruns. According to the Baseball Reference website, here what "typical" seasons for both players looked like:

> Perez .279 avg, .341 obp, .463 slug, 22 hr, 96 rbi,
>   74 runs
> Allen .292 avg, .378 obp, .534 slug, 33 hr, 104 rbi,
>   102 runs

As an every-day player, Dick Allen was clearly better than Perez. The genial Cuban, Perez, who spent most of his career with the Reds, added to his lifetime stats by playing several seasons at the tail end as a part-timer, including one year with the Phillies (1983).

Perez does get points for being an important part of some outstanding ball clubs, but should Dick Allen be penalized because his fate was to play for more mediocre teams? It's hard to imagine the 1964 Phillies almost winning the pennant without Allen in the lineup. And in 1972, Allen's performance helped lift the White Sox into playoff contention.

The purpose of this comparison is not to diminish the fine career of Tony Perez. He was a gamer and one of baseball's best clutch hitters. He deserves to be in the Hall of Fame. But if he does, so does Dick Allen.

A typical Allen season also compares favorably to other Hall of Famers who played first/third and played about 15 years. The power numbers for Frank Chance and Jimmy Collins are low because they played during an era when the balls weren't as lively as they would be later in the twentieth century. It was harder to hit homeruns back then:

George Kell (15 years) .306 avg, .367 obp, .414 slug,
7 hr, 79 rbi, 79 runs

Frank Chance (17 years) .296 avg, .394 obp,
.394 slug, 3 hr, 75 rbi, 100 runs

Jimmy Collins (14 years) .294 avg, .343 obp,
.409 slug, 6 hr, 92 rbi, 99 runs

Dick Allen (15 years) .292 avg, .378 obp, .534 slug,
33 hr, 104 rbi, 102 runs

David Fleming points out at Bill James Online that Dick Allen was the best hitter in baseball over a ten-year period, using the "adjusted on-base-plus-slugging" stat (obs+). Here are the obs+ numbers for players between 1964 and 1973 (Allen's prime). Seventeen Hall of Famers played 1000 or more games during those ten years. Dick Allen had a better obs+ than all of them, and there are some pretty good names on the list:

Name	obs+
Dick Allen	165
Hank Aaron	161
Willie McCovey	161
Frank Robinson	161
Harmon Killebrew	152
Willie Stargell	152
Roberto Clemente	151

Willie Mays	148
Frank Howard	147
Carl Yastrzemski	145
Al Kaline	140
Boog Powell	140
Billy Williams	139
Tony Oliva	137
Ron Santo	136

As Fleming concludes: "Dick Allen really was the best hitter in baseball, for a span of ten years."

—

So, Dick Allen was one of the premier sluggers of his era and racked-up numbers equal-to or better-than many who are already in the Hall of Fame. The main stumbling block to his candidacy seems to be the rap that he was a troublemaking bad boy who caused problems in the clubhouse. Even if this was true (and there are many who played alongside Allen who said this was not the case), since when is a bad-boy image criteria for exclusion from baseball's immortals? Ty Cobb, Rogers Hornsby, and even Ted Williams were all self-absorbed jerks at times. Those troubled souls are in the Hall of Fame and nobody asks why.

(And let's not even get into the steroid-era debate. Imagine what Allen would have done if he had been on the juice, which he never was.)

My argument is that—based on the statistics alone—Number 15 earned a spot in the Hall of Fame. And if I can be allowed to use the old eyeball test, he was one of the greatest players I ever saw…and I've been watching major league baseball for over 50 years.

CHAPTER 7

One-Year Wonders

"Where have you gone, Joe DiMaggio? A nation turns its lonely eyes to you, wo wo wo. What's that you say, Mrs. Robinson. 'Joltin Joe' has left and gone away, hey hey hey. Hey hey hey." – Simon and Garfunkel

———

Many of the greatest players in baseball, such as Joe DiMaggio and others, have long, storied careers. But here are two that didn't, but they coulda, shoulda, woulda.

How many seasons would you expect an outfielder to play after hitting .313 and finishing fourth in the National League homerun race during his rookie season? Barring injury, most would say that player had a bright future in the big leagues. Ten to fifteen years of solid production would not be an unreasonable statistical projection. The actual major league career of outfielder Buzz Arlett defies that conventional wisdom. Playing for the Philadelphia Phillies in

1931, the right-hand-hitting outfielder smacked 18 homeruns, stroked seven triples, drove in 72 runs, and slugged at a .537 clip. Yet, he played in the minor leagues in 1932 and for years afterwards.

What happened? Well, first of all, Arlett was already 32 years old when he broke in with the Philadelphia Phillies. He had spent the previous 13 seasons with the minor league Oakland Oaks of the old Pacific Coast League, racking up great numbers. Over those 13 seasons, Arlett compiled league records 251 homeruns and 1135 rbi.

The totals assuredly would have been much higher had Buzz not spent the first five years of his career almost exclusively as a pitcher (108-93, 3.42 era). It was as a hurler that Arlett received the nickname "Buzz"; it apparently referred to his ability to "buzz" through opposing lineups.

But it was Arlett's prodigious offensive production earned him the moniker "The Babe Ruth of the Minor Leagues." This was not faint praise, as the minor leagues of this era, in particular the Pacific Coast League, were strong and competed aggressively with the major leagues for the best players. The minors' descent into secondary status didn't begin until Branch Rickey's tenure in the 1930s with the Cardinals.

In 1930, the year before Arlett's longer-than-a-cup-of-coffee (my fifth and final cliché) with the Phillies, he hit .374 for the Oaks and drove in 189 runs. Suitably impressed, the Phils signed him in the off-season and dreamed of the offensive devastation he would cause in a lineup that also featured sluggers Chuck Klein and Don Hurst. However, they failed to take into account Arlett's defensive weaknesses and how his brutal outfield play would adversely affect an already beleaguered Phillies pitching staff (4.58 team era in 1931).

Arlett had been a decent defensive player earlier in his career, but by the time he arrived in Philadelphia his weight had ballooned from 185 to 230 pounds. The added girth made him slow and ponderous, something the Phillies didn't need in their ongoing efforts to chase down the frequent long flies and gappers in the Baker Bowl.

So, even though his offensive numbers were better-than-good, Arlett and the Phillies parted ways after the 1931 season. He returned to the minors for six more years and continued to be an offensive force. As a member of the old Baltimore Orioles of the International League, Arlett twice hit four homeruns in a single game. In 1933 and 1934, he hit 39 and 41 homeruns, respectively.

He retired in 1937 at the age of thirty-eight. His final minor league stats included 432 homeruns, a .341 career batting average, and a .604 slugging percentage. Had he spent a few more seasons in the majors, Arlett probably would be remembered today. Maybe he'd even be mentioned in a popular song. We know that the minors of his era were loaded with great players, and there's no reason to believe he would not have continued to be a fine offensive player in the National or American League. But then there was that defense...and those extra pounds. There's only one thing that can't be denied: Buzz Arlett only played one year in the major leagues, even though he hit like crazy.

—

Herb Washington has the distinction of being major league baseball's most-famous pinch runner. A year after the American League installed the "Designated Hitter" rule to enable another player to bat in place of the pitcher, Washington's role on the Oakland A's was tagged by the fans and the media as that of a "Designated Runner." Twenty-two other players in baseball history have had careers as mainly pinch runners, but Washington played under the spotlight of one of baseball's then-best teams, a club owned by a flamboyant owner who garnered a lot of publicity. The media coverage he received while playing for Charles Finley insured a degree of notoriety and fame.

The speedy Mississippi native began his major league career with the A's on April 4, 1974, and appeared in 92 games that year, all as a pinch runner. He swiped 29 bases and scored 29 runs for an A's club that won the American League Western Division.

Washington's stolen base percentage that year was 64.9%, not bad but not the high Maury Wills/Lou Brock/Ty Cobb type of figure that Finley had been hoping for. In addition, the A's owner was less than pleased when Washington was picked off base during the 1974 World Series against the Los Angeles Dodgers (even though the A's won the series in five games). After appearing in just 13 games in 1975 with just two steals (out of three attempts), Finley tired of the experiment and released Washington on May 4, after a grand total of 105 games in the majors.

Washington has been one active dude since his brief stint with the A's. He ran track professionally for a couple of years before trading in his running gear for business attire and a brief case. Drafted to play football by the Baltimore Colts prior to his tenure with the A's, he might have opted to give pro football a try after being released by Oakland. Nicknamed "Hurricane" because of his blazing speed, Washington had the potential to become a deep threat receiver in the NFL. Instead, he ended up opening a McDonald's restaurant franchise in one of the poorest areas of Rochester, New York. His decision to establish one of the chain's eateries in a section of town that others considered extremely high-risk met with outstanding success. Within a few years Washington had opened several more "Mickey D's" in Rochester, and he eventually acquired franchises in Pennsylvania.

As time went by, Washington built a reputation for being an astute business person. The

Federal Reserve Bank of Buffalo noticed the one-time track star's financial acumen and in 1992 elevated him to the chairmanship of its board of directors. Later, Washington was named a director of the Federal Reserve Bank of New York, making him one of the most influential black individuals at the time in the world of high finance.

Washington's post-baseball activities have also included personal involvement in the United Way, the Urban League, and the New York State Athletic Association. Plus, he founded the Youngstown Steelhounds pro hockey team in 2005.

So, what do you think? That's an impressive resume for a guy whose baseball career is considered at best an anomaly and at worst a joke, isn't it? As a young man, Herb Washington proved he could run with the best of them. Over the years, he proved it again and again and again.

Chapter 8

See You
in September

"Baseball is drama with an endless run and an ever-changing cast." – Joe Garagiola

———

Every September 1, all major league baseball teams are permitted to expand their rosters from 25 to 40 players. Older players who are looking for another crack at the big show are sometimes called up for possible playing time. But this expansion is mostly used to give talented young players who have toiled in the minors all season some plate appearances or mound time against major league competition.

It's one thing to tear up AAA pitching, but can the minor league slugger handle a big-league curve? Blowing away hitters in places such as Hagerstown, Norfolk, or Scranton is easy for some pitchers, but can he throw that fastball past an eight-year major league veteran who's hitting .324?

September call-ups can answer a lot of questions for some players and lead to productive careers. Some of the great stars of the last 40 years have proven their readiness for the Big Show by playing well after being summoned to the majors for the last month of the regular season. Here are seven of them, all from the modern era.

—

In September 1971, 20-year-old Greg Luzinski (who started out by crushing balls through the windows of the homes surrounding Notre Dame High School for Boys in Niles, Illinois) impressed the Phillies by hitting .300 for the major league team and driving in 15 runs in 100 at-bats. "The Bull" would go on to have seasons in which he powered 29, 34, 39, and 35 homeruns for Philly. As a member of the White Sox in 1983, Luzinski hit 32 round-trippers, including one of the longest balls ever hit at old Comiskey Park.

—

On September 8, 1972, pitcher Steve Busby

took the mound for the first time for the Kansas City Royals. Making the most of his opportunity, the righty went 3-1 with a 1.58 era over the last month of the season. In 40 innings of work, Busby only allowed 28 hits. This success was a harbinger of great things to come; Busby would win 22 games in 1973 and 18 in 1974, including a no-hitter each season. Knee and rotator-cuff injuries shortened this talented pitcher's career. He retired after the 1980 season with a life-time record of 70-54.

—

Red Sox outfielder Fred Lynn clearly showed that he had what it takes during his September 1974 call-up. In 43 at-bats, Lynn hit a sizzling .419, drilled a couple of homers, and knocked in ten runs. Proving this performance was no fluke, Lynn went on to hit .331 for the 1975 BoSox and snared both Rookie-of-the-Year and MVP awards honors. Lynn was the first player ever to accomplish that feat. (Ichiro Suzuki did so with the Seattle Mariners in 2001, but he was much older that Lynn was when he made it to the majors and had played professional ball for many years in Japan.) In 17 years as a major leaguer, the Chicago native Lynn was named to nine American League All-Star teams.

—

The man nicknamed "El Toro" made an impressive debut in September 1980 for the Dodgers. At the age of 19, pitcher Fernando Valenzuela baffled hitters for a 0.00 era over 17.2 innings of work. Along with two wins, Valenzuela saved a game and set the stage for his simultaneous Rookie-of-the-Year and Cy Young awards in 1981 (the only pitcher to have ever received this honor).

—

Los Angeles also gave pitcher Tim Belcher the call in September of 1987. His 4-2, 2.38 performance convinced Dodgers brass that the righty was ready and made him a part of their rotation in 1988. He responded with 12 wins and an era below 3.00; in five years with the Dodgers, Belcher averaged nearly 162 innings pitched and won 50 games. The 6'3" hurler pitched for six different teams before retiring in 2000.

—

Outfielder J.D. Drew made his debut in September of 1997 for St Louis, and what a debut it was! Cardinal fans thrilled to watch the 22-year-old blast five homeruns and hit .417 in 41 plate appearances. Drew, who would go on to hit 242 homers over a 14-year career, also led league right fielders in fielding percentage in 2004, 2009, and 2010.

—

Eventual closer-extraordinaire Eric Gagne first took the mound in the major leagues on September 7, 1999, for the Dodgers. The 23-year-old Canadian blew away 30 batters on strikeouts in 30 innings of work while posting a miniscule 2.10 era. However, Gagne didn't become a premier door-slammer right away. The Dodgers used him as a starter in 2000 and 2001 with so-so results (10-13 overall record) before moving him to the bullpen in 2002. Smart move! Gagne saved 52 games in 2002, 55 in 2003, and 45 in 2004 for the Dodgers—with earned run averages of 1.97, 1.20 and 2.19 respectively. His work in 2003 earned him the National League's Cy Young Award. Injuries would limit Gagne's effectiveness after 2004, and he wrapped up his career by posting a poor 5.44 era for the Brewers in 2008. But for a time, the guy who did so well in September of 1999 was one of baseball's best.

—

Luzinski, Busby, Lynn, Valenzuela, Belcher, Drew, and Gagne showed that a hot September call-up often is a good indicator of future success. Not always true, but often enough to make it worth paying attention in the fall, whether your team is in contention or not.

CHAPTER 9

How the Heck Did This Team Finish Last?

"I come to play! I come to beat you! I come to kill you!"
– Leo Duroucher

———

Here's the story of another "good" team that stunk it up one season. It might be a good thing for Cubs fans to remember this story after their heady World Championship of 2016.

When the Chicago Cubs finished last in 2012, it marked the first time in 46 years that the franchise had ended a season in the basement.

A lot of us forgot that fact as we talked about the "curse" and the "drought." But in 1966, the Cubbies finished tenth in a ten-team league with the following pretty-good starting position players:

C Randy Hundley (4th, 1966 Rookie-of-the-Year vote)

1B Ernie Banks (.272 avg, 15 HR, 75 rbi)

2B Glen Beckert (.287 avg, 59 rbi)

3B Ron Santo (.312 avg, 30 HR, 94 rbi)

SS Don Kessinger (.274 avg)

LF Byron Browne (.243 avg, 16 HR)

CF Adolfo Phillips (.262 avg, 16 HR)

RF Billy Williams (.276 avg, 29 HR, 91 rbi)

Chicago featured three future Hall of Famers (Banks, Santo, and Williams) playing every day, plus a four-time All Star at second base (Beckert). Don Kessinger was a fine shortstop who could hit, and the outfield of Browne, Phillips, and Williams slugged 61 long balls between them. The Cub position players' seasonal stats weren't eye popping, but they were above average.

So how did this club finish behind the then-woeful Mets and Astros?

—

The starting rotation looks like it belonged to anything but a last place team. Most managers would have loved to start the season with a staff that included Dick Ellsworth, Ken Holtzman, Bill Hands, and Ernie Broglio/Fergie Jenkins.

All five logged some outstanding seasons in their careers, but in 1966 Ellsworth lost 22 games, Hands logged an era of 4.58, and Broglio allowed a whopping 6.35 earned runs per nine innings pitched. Holtzman was a bright spot, winning 11 games on a team that only won 59, as was the future Hall of Famer Jenkins. The lanky Canadian came over from the Phillies during the season and posted a decent 3.31 average while striking out 148 batters in 182 innings.

But even a starting lineup that included Babe Ruth, Ty Cobb, and Hank Aaron (or Anthony Rizzo, Kris Bryant, and Kyle Schwarber, for that matter) would have had trouble winning a lot of games with the 1966 Cubs pitching staff. Along with some of the starters having off years, the bullpen was mediocre at best. Closer Bob Hendley saved only six games and surrendered 98 hits in 89.2 innings of work. Cal Koonce was okay with a 5-5 record and a 3.81 era, but Bill Hoeft (4.61 era) and Ted Abernathy (6.18 era) were no help at all.

For the season, the Cubs pitchers finished last in era, last in hits allowed, last in runs allowed, and last in homeruns allowed.

—

The Chicago pitchers might have fared a little better had their fielders caught a few more balls. Over the course of the 1966 campaign, the team finished eighth (out of ten clubs) in fielding percentage. And that was before Bill James and John Dewan and Ben Jedlovec of Sports Info Solutions began revolutionizing the process of identifying, collecting, and analyzing all the new defensive stats that now populate (some say overpopulate) the game.

So even though the Cubs had a good starting lineup in 1966, it was largely pitching and, to a lesser extent, fielding that let them down.

—

In 1967, the Cubs improved by 28 games, jumping from tenth to third place. One of the big reasons for the improvement was Fergie Jenkins' emergence as a premier starting pitcher (20 wins, 2.80 era). In addition, manager Leo Durocher got good seasons from young pitchers Rich Nye (13 wins, 3.20 era) and Joe Niekro (10 wins, 3.34 era).

The starting lineup continued to produce offensively, finishing first in the league in runs scored, and the Cubs suddenly began to make the defensive plays major league teams are supposed to make, finishing first in fielding with an outstanding .981 fielding percentage.

The Cubs were on the way up and would field good-excellent teams for the next several years. Of course, then came the collapse of 1969 to the Amazin' Mets. At a quick glance, though, it's puzzling how the 1966 team finished with a record of 59-103. But if you look a little closer, it's clear what happened: You have to keep the other guys from scoring more runs than you do to get to raise that "W" flag over Wrigley Field so the commuters on their way home from work on the El can see who won!

CHAPTER 10

The Hitless Wonders Won It All

"The world is full of magic things, patiently waiting for our senses to grow sharper." – W.B. Yeats

———

The 1906 Chicago White Sox hit a meager .230 as a team and won the American League pennant. Then, they rolled a powerful Cubs team in six games to win the World Series. How did they do it, I wondered. So I did a little research.

Offensively, the 1906 White Sox lineup wasn't exactly an early version of the 1927 Yankees "Murderers Row" or even the Cubs team of 2016:

Billy Sullivan C	.214 avg, .262 obp
Jiggs Donahue 1B	.257 avg, .320 obp
Frank Isbell 2B	.279 avg, .324 obp
George Davis SS	.277 avg, .338 obp
Lee Tannehill 3B	.183 avg, .254 obp
Bill O'Neill OF	.248 avg, .301 obp
Ed Hahn OF	.227 avg, .335 obp
Fielder Jones OF	.230 avg, .346 obp

On the bench, player-manager Fielder Jones had guys that hit .258, .233, .196, and .135 respectively. Along with compiling the lowest team batting average in the league, the pennant-winning White Sox also finished last in hits, homeruns, slugging percentage, and total bases. Even though this was during baseball's "dead-ball" era, a time when batting averages were at historic lows, the White Sox were a poor hitting team. The last-place Boston Americans hit seven points higher as a club and registered almost 100 more base hits over the course of the 1906 campaign than the Sox.

—

Dubbed the "Hitless Wonders" by the Chicago press, the White Sox were, however, blessed with a dominant array of pitching. Led by 22-game winner Frank Owen and 20-game winner Nick Altrock, the team's earned run average for 1906 was a miniscule 2.13.

After facing staff aces Owen and Altrock, league batters had to face Ed Walsh (1.88 era), Doc White (1.52 era), and Roy Patterson (2.09 era). White Sox pitchers allowed the fewest number of earned runs (460) and were the stingiest in the league in allowing free passes (255).

The eventual World Champs may not have been getting their hits but the opposition was having an even tougher time getting on-base in their turn at bat.

—

So, outstanding pitching was the main reason why the White Sox won the pennant and World Series in 1906. But to win games, a team needs to score at least a few runs, and the Southsiders did some other things well to compensate for their lack of hitting punch. For starters, they were a hustling team that played smart. They were opportunistic, swiping 216 bases, good for third in the league, an incredible number considering the team's overall anemic hitting. The 1906 White Sox were also patient at the plate, leading the American League in walks. And they weren't afraid to "take one for the club" and led the Junior Circuit in hit batsmen.

The White Sox finished second in the league with a .963 fielding percentage, so they weren't killing themselves by making a lot of bonehead plays on defense. When it came to all the intangibles, it looks like they were a determined bunch that didn't give an inch or let up for a second on the field.

—

The White Sox got out of the gate slowly in 1906 and were 7.5 games out of first at the end of July. An incredible 19-game winning streak in August moved them into first place; after a tough September race with Cleveland and New York, the Chicago team crossed the finish line as league champs, three games over the New York Highlanders.

No one gave the Sox much of a chance to beat the cross-town Cubs in the 1906 World Series. (In fact, the Cubs went on to win back-to-back World Championships in 1907 and 1908, becoming the first team to play in three World Series in a row and the first to win two in a row. Of course, we know what happened for the next 108 years.) Backed by potent hitting and outstanding pitching, the Cubbies roared to a 116-36 record for an all-time-best winning percentage of .763, a record that still stands. The White Sox finished with an excellent 93-58 record, but nobody gave them a chance against the potent Westsiders (the Cubs didn't move to the north side of Chicago until 1916).

—

However, the Cub juggernaut never materialized. Despite the fact that the White Sox only hit .097 in the first four games of the Series, they hustled and scratched their way a couple of wins. In game five, helped by new ground rules at the Cubs' West Side Park, the White Sox smacked several doubles into the roped-off standing-room-only crowd that ringed the outfield and won 8-6.

In the sixth game, the Sox rocked a tired Mordecai "Three Finger" Brown (who had already pitched two complete games in the Series and would later be elected to the Hall of Fame) and beat the shocked Cubs 8-3 to win it all.

Now, it is said that hubris probably played a large part in the Cubs' downfall. After all, just about everyone who followed baseball expected them to crush their weak-hitting opponents. But the White Sox had certain strengths (great pitching, good defense, sound fundamental skills, a fierce determination to win) and kept hustling like they had done all season long. No one had expected them to win the pennant, either, remember. I see this series as a story about how baseball is not always about hits, but it is always about wonder.

—

When the dust cleared, late in the afternoon of October 19, 1906, the Chicago White Sox were World Champions. Not a bad ending for a bunch of hitless wonders. The Sox went on to win the World Series in 1917 (against the Giants) and in 2005 (against the Houston Astros), and they beat the New York Yankees for the AL pennant in 1959 but lost the World Series to the Los Angeles Dodgers in six games. The only other time the White Sox made it into the World Series was in 1919, but that is the subject of the next story in this book.

CHAPTER 11

Mob or No Mob

"It is never too late to be what you might have been."
— George Eliot

———

The Indians of 2016 certainly could have beaten the Cubs in the World Series, curse or no curse. And so, I will argue, could the other team from Ohio, the Cincinnati Reds, have beaten the Chicago White Sox in 1919, mob or no mob.

Major League baseball was shaken to its foundation that year when eight players on the White Sox conspired to throw the 1919 World Series. Conventional wisdom now says the "Black Sox" would have blown away an inferior team like the Reds had key players on Chicago not been in cahoots with gamblers. The idea that the Reds were not nearly as good as the Sox is often cited as one of the evidences for a fix.

But sometimes conventional wisdom can be wrong. And it's wrong when it comes to analyzing the two teams involved in the infamous 1919 World Series.

—

The 1919 Chicago White Sox were a very good ball club, don't get me wrong. Led by rookie Manager Kid Gleason, they finished with an outstanding 88-52 record and led the American League in hitting with a .287 team average. The starting lineup featured superstars "Shoeless" Joe Jackson (.351 avg, 96 rbi), Eddie Collins (.319 avg, 80 rbi, 33 steals), and four other regulars who hit between .290 and .302.

However, the National League Reds had won eight more games (96 total) than the Sox during the regular season with a lineup that featured all-time greats such as outfielder Ed Roush (.321 avg) and third baseman Heinie Groh (.310 avg). Roush and Groh's supporting cast included four guys who hit between .264 and .276.

From an offensive standpoint, the White Sox were better on paper but the Reds weren't bad and had enough bullets in their gun to win a short (albeit eight-game) World Series.

The widely-held belief that the Chicago team

was much better than Cincinnati falls flat when you compare pitching staffs. The White Sox were led by Eddie Ciotte who won 29 games and posted a microscopic 1.82 era. Others having good years were Lefty Williams (23-11, 2.64) and Dickey Kerr (13-7, 2.88). The staff as a whole finished fourth in the American League with 3.04 era—not bad but not exactly over-powering.

—

According to the statistics, the Reds had a much better pitching staff than the Sox in 1919. Cincy's composite earned-run-average was a sparkling 2.23 compared to 3.04 for Chicago, and their pitchers also bested the White Sox in the following important categories:

Runs Allowed: Reds 401, White Sox 534
Walks Allowed: Reds 298, White Sox 342
Homeruns Allowed: Reds 21, White Sox 24
WHIP: Reds 1.100, White Sox 1.254

Cincinnati's pitchers also hurled more shutouts during the regular season than Chicago (23-14). Along with 21-game winner Slim Salee, manager Pat Moran had Hod Eller (19-9, 2.39 era),

Dutch Reuther (19-6, 1.82 era), Ray Fisher (14-5, 2.17 era), and Dolf Luque (10-3, 2.63 era) at his disposal during the 1919 campaign. And the Reds were a better fielding team during the regular season with a .974 percentage compared to .969 for the White Sox.

—

So, there can be no argument that Cincinnati had a superior pitching staff and a better fielding team going into the 1919 Fall Classic. The White Sox did have a better hitting club, but it wasn't like they were facing a team of Mario Mendozas in the Reds. Based on the numbers, it's puzzling why the experts expected such a Chicago rout.

Sure, the White Sox did have Ciotte, who had an incredible year on the mound. He would have started at least twice, perhaps three times. Had Eddie been on the level, Chicago had a great chance to capture the championship. Over the years, it's been shown time and time again that one or two great pitchers can take any team a long way in the postseason.

But the Reds had excellent pitchers such as Salee, Eller, Ruether, and others. Chicago may have had an edge for having Ciotte, but it wasn't an insurmountable one. Perhaps the odds-makers were swayed in their thinking by the fact that the American League had won eight of the previous nine World Series. It looked like the AL was becoming dominant and 1919 was simply going to continue that trend.

Giving those that were alive at the time and saw these players perform the benefit of the doubt, perhaps the White Sox were a better team. Maybe the American League was superior back then. It's very possible that an honest Ed Ciotte—backed by equally honest teammates— would have been enough to handily defeat the Reds in the World Series. But we'll never be allowed to know.

The Reds had better pitchers. They played the field better. They had guys that could hit. Maybe they didn't need anyone's help to beat the "Black Sox." Based on the statistics, it seems to me at least a reasonable possibility that the Ohio team could have beat the Illinois team both times—1919 and 2016—without the fix or despite the curse.

Coulda. Woulda. Shoulda.

CHAPTER 12

When Baseball Was Really Baseball

*"Figures often beguile me, particularly when I have
the arranging of them myself; in which case the remark
attributed to Disraeli would often apply with justice and
force: "There are three kinds of lies: lies, damned lies,
and statistics."* – Mark Twain

Not long ago, I was rooting through some boxes
in my attic when I discovered an old open-reel
tape. The spool was dusty and slightly lop-sided
and the tape itself was quite brittle. Curious
about what had been recorded, I called a dear
friend who collected old radios and tape players
and asked if I could use one of his machines.

"Return the garden spreader you borrowed
three years ago and something can be arranged,"
he said. I agreed to his terms and made an ap-
pointment to listen to my discovery.

To my amazement, the tape contained the oral autobiography of my great-grandfather, Jacob Jeremiah. "Jake" Jeremiah played professional baseball at the beginning of the 1900s. I estimate that the recording dates back to 1960 or so. I never met my great-grandfather but had heard many stories about him. After listening to his recollections, I feel I know him better and understand his era more clearly.

What follows is a transcript of the tape. When finished, I hope you'll share my conviction that my great-grandfather's story beautifully capsulizes the days when baseball was really baseball.

—

My name is Jacob Jeremiah and I used to play baseball. They called me 'Jake,' that's a nickname you know, and I was an infielder when I wasn't playing the outfield or catching. I even pitched a few times and once tossed against the great Cy Young. It was a scoreless battle until they came to the dish.

HA HA HA.

Just a little joke there, to let you know we ballplayers have a sense of humor. We had to, the little bit of money they gave us to play. My first team was the Moulstown (Pennsylvania) Mosquitoes in the old Pigeon Hills League. I had to kick back five bucks a month to the manager to be on the team!

I didn't mind; it was 1898 and I was glad to be playing ball and not sweating in the town shoe factory, cutting out tongues all day.

The Mosquitoes were good; we played hard but weren't out for blood like some of the other fellows. Some of the other teams sharpened their spikes before each game. You had to be careful playing the infield back in those days.

At one point, the Mosquitoes won 67 or 68 games in a row. We played double headers every day and two twin bills on Saturday. The pro teams started to notice and four of us ended up in the big leagues; me, Mordecai Wood, Rube Stolzfus, and Dutch Germany. I broke in with the Philadelphia National League club.

—

I was very grateful, you know, to get my monthly paycheck of ten dollars. I was making a third of that at the shoe factory and as a ballplayer we got all the baked beans and brown bread we could eat. Izzy, our team cook, stirred us up a batch every day and that's what we ate. On the road trips, sometimes they wouldn't have to coal-stoke the trains until we were halfway to St. Louis or Pittsburgh.

The windows had three little screens to keep the coal ashes out of the cars, but sometimes an ember would make its way in and burn you. As a matter of fact, you weren't considered part of the club until your clothes were set on fire. Most of the guys would help you put out the flames, and you didn't complain about a thing like that, you know? You were glad to be a ballplayer.

I don't know if I should mention this, but I heard that Ty Cobb used to squirt FLIT on his teammates when they started to smolder. Could be just a rumor, but I'm glad I never played for the Tigers.

—

Today, all the players seem to be swinging for a home-run. Good night! I didn't see a ball go over the fence until I was twenty-five years old and that was during an exhibition game in Cuba in the middle of a hurricane!

Baseball was baseball then. In the old Philadelphia ballpark the left field fence was nothing but chicken wire and was 545 feet from home plate. Once, I saw Maxie Trone rip a long one to left that hit a wet spot and skidded under the wire. Then it rolled almost a quarter mile to Fairmont Park. Ground rules were kind of fuzzy back then, so that ball was in play. The outfielder hopped a passing trolley to make time. Maxie was a true old-timer and believed in real baseball, so he stopped at third base, even though he could have circled the bags a dozen times. He wasn't going to have an "inside the park" homerun if the ball wasn't actually inside the park! Baseball needs more Maxie Trones, fellows who keep the homerun in its rightful perspective.

—

During my career, I played against many of the greats. I remember the day I met Honus Wagner. He was one of the nicest guys in baseball and had just accidentally plunked me in the back with a ball during warmups.

"Hey," he said good-naturedly, "don't walk between us when we're having a catch."

"Busher!' his warm-up partner said. I smiled and picked up the ball.

"You mind if I keep this?" I asked. I wanted a souvenir for my grandchildren.

With a twinkle in his eye, the Flying Dutchman

walked up to me and placed his huge hands on my shoulders. "Keep it, you slacker, and I'll rip out your esophagus."

We all had a nice chuckle and I gave him back the ball. Later in the game, he spiked me as I went into second base. We had another laugh over that, and then I clocked him.

—

My lifetime batting average was only .229, but I did manage to hit only one homerun in 17 years. That was back in the Dead Ball Era. Once in Brooklyn, we were out of fresh balls and ended up borrowing some cannon balls from the local armory. Nobody noticed the difference, although a couple of the fans were taken to hospitals when they tried to catch a foul ball.

Because I wasn't much of a hitter, I tried to make up for it by being a whirlygig on the bases. I stole over 300 bases in my career. That was baseball! Get on base and steal! Sometimes, I'd even try to steal second base after striking out. Only one umpire worked the games back then, and he couldn't keep his eyes on everything, so I'd fly straight across the mound and dive headfirst into second base. Yep, those were the days!

Toward the end of my career, I got sold to Hackensack (New Jersey) in the old Eastern Mojave League. That was the year the Great War broke out and President Wilson needed plenty of red-blooded American boys to fight the Kaiser. Players were scarce and we took anybody who had a glove and spikes. In Hackensack, our center fielder was named Leapy Lyons, and he was all heart. You see, Leapy was confined to an iron lung and didn't catch many balls. But he sure was an inspiration!

When the war ended, the real baseball players started to come home, and I started to think about my future. Not having the soul to get back into the shoe business, I asked my manager for some advice. "Hey, Buck-a-roo," I said. "What should I do about my career?" Since my average was down to .168, I thought it was a reasonable question.

After telling me to never call him 'Buck-a-roo' again, he shifted his wad of chewing tobacco from cheek to cheek and scratched his groin. "Jeremiah," he said, spitting brown tobacco juice on my spikes. "Your batting eye is gone, you can't run, and you're losing your hair. You stink at baseball and you also stink from not taking your showers regularly. There's only one thing for you to do. Become an umpire."

Considering my declining skills and the fact that

he had just ruined my only pair of spikes, it was good advice. The next spring I enrolled in umpire school. Money was tight, I hadn't saved a cent, so I learned my balls and strikes during the day and took a job teaching Braille to some of my colleagues-in-blue at night. I umped for twenty years after that. In 1939, me and my guide dog, One-Eyed Willie, retired with full pension benefits of $10 a month.

—

That's about it. All-in-all, I've had a good life and I'm mighty proud to have been a part of baseball when baseball was really baseball. I've done a lot of fishing since. Mostly fresh water when I can find any. Occasionally, I'll drive down to Philly and watch a game. It's nice, but I wish they'd stop hitting so many balls over the fence.

Sources

Bookend Buddies

National Sun Times website article dated 12/24/205 "Anthony Rizzo and Kris Bryant are serious bros": http://national.suntimes.com/mlb/7/72/2339673/anthony-rizzo-kris-bryant-best-friends/.

USA Today website article dated 11/3/2016 "Best buds Anthony Rizzo, Kris Bryant help lift Cubs to long-awaited title": http://www.usatoday.com/story/sports/mlb/2016/11/03/best-buds-rizzo-bryant-help-lift-cubs-to-long-awaited-title/93226662/.

World History Project website article on the 1926 World Series": https://worldhistoryproject.org/1926/10/2/1926-world-series.

How Stuff Works website article "Babe Ruth and Lou Gehrig": http://entertainment.howstuffworks.com/babe-ruth31.htm.

SB Nation website article dated July 8, 2014 "75 years later, Babe Ruth's hug means almost as much as Lou Gehrig's speech": http://www.sbnation.com/mlb/2014/7/8/5878847/lou-gehrig-babe-ruth-75-anniversary-luckiest-man-speech-forgiveness-history.

New York Times website article "Ruth and Gehrig: Forced Smiles" dated 6-2-1991: http://www.nytimes.com/1991/06/02/sports/baseball-ruth-and-gehrig-forced-smiles.html.

Baseball Reference website pages on Bryant, Rizzo, Ruth, Gehrig; 1926 New York Yankees; 1926 World Series; 2016 Chicago Cubs; 2016 World Series; 1908 World Series.

Curse or No Curse

History Channel website article "How a Billy Goat 'Cursed' the Chicago Cubs" by Evan Andrews dated 9-24-15: http://www.history.com/news/how-a-billy-goat-cursed-the-chicago-cubs.

Sporting News website article "Cubs' curse is alive and well at the Billy Goat Tavern" by Ryan Fagan dated 10-18-16: http://www.sportingnews.com/mlb/news/mlb-playoffs-2016-billy-goat-curse-nlcs-chicago-cubs-dodgers-bartman-black-cat/14ds1v2mohrrg1s20y9pucknky.

About Sports website page about famous baseball curses compiled by Scott Kendrick dated 8-25-16: http://baseball.about.com/od/majorleaguehistory/tp/baseballcurses.htm.

Reading Eagle website article "Will the Indians End the 'Curse' of Rocky Colavito?" by Brian Smith dated

10-29-16: http://www.readingeagle.com/sports/article/will-indians-end-the-curse-of-rocky-colavito#.WIQXHVMrLIU.

Baseball Reference website 2016 Chicago Cubs statistics page: http://www.baseball-reference.com/teams/CHC/2016.shtml.

Baseball Reference website 2016 Cleveland Indians statistics page: http://www.baseball-reference.com/teams/CLE/2016.shtml.

From the Penthouse to the Outhouse

Baseball Reference website 1965 New York Yankees statistics page.

Baseball Reference website 1964 New York Yankees statistics page.

Baseball Almanac website 1965 Yankees page.

Baseball Almanac website 1964 Yankees page.

When the Mets Became Amazin'

The New Bill James Historical Baseball Abstract, Bill James, Free Press 2003.

The Baseball Encyclopedia, Simon and Schuster 1996.

Baseball Reference website 1969 New York Mets statistics page.

Baseball Almanac website 1969 Mets page.

All Music website Jerry Reed bio by Jason Ankeny:http://www.allmusic.com/artist/jerry-reed-mn0000334644.

Baseball Reference website1969 Chicago Cubs statistics page: http://www.baseball-reference.com/teams/CHC/1969.shtml.

Baseball Almanac website1969 Cubs page: http://www.baseball-almanac.com/teamstats/roster.php?y=1969&t=CHN.

My First Baseball Thrill

Baseball Reference website 1967 Major League baseball season re-cap.

Baseball Almanac website 1967 baseball season, day-by-day page.

NOAA website: summary and photos of 1967's "Hurricane Doria."

The New Phillies Encyclopedia, Bilovsky and Westcott, Temple University Press 1993.

The author's own first-hand recollections of the event.

Should Dick Allen Be in the Hall of Fame?

The New Phillies Encyclopedia, Bilovsky and Westcott, Temple University Press 1993.

The New Bill James Historical Baseball Abstract, Bill James, Free Press 2003.

September Swoon, William C. Kashhatus, Keystone Books 2004.

Baseball Reference website Dick Allen career statistics page.

The Baseball Encyclopedia, Simon and Schuster 1996.

One-Year Wonders

The New Phillies Encyclopedia, Bilovsky and Westcott, Temple University Press 1993.

The New Bill James Historical Baseball Abstract, Bill James, Free Press 2003

Society for American Baseball Research website "Buzz Arlett" profile by Cort Vitty.

The Philadelphia Phillies, Donald Honig, Simon and Schuster 1992.

The Baseball Encyclopedia, Simon and Schuster 1996.

S.F. Gate website "Where Are They Now?/Herb Washington" by Jorge L. Ortiz posted January 13, 2002.

Baseball Reference website biographical information on Herb Washington in the "BR Bullpen."

Society For American Baseball Research website article about Herb Washington: http://sabr.org/bio-proj/person/00ad7a34.

See You in September

The Baseball Encyclopedia, Simon and Schuster 1996.

Baseball Reference website various player pages.

Baseball Almanac website various player pages.

The New Bill James Historical Baseball Abstract, Bill James, Free Press 2003.

How Did This Team End Up Last?

Baseball Reference website Chicago Cubs 1966 statistics page.

Baseball Reference website: Chicago Cubs 1967 statistics page.

Baseball Almanac website Cubs 1966 page.

Baseball Almanac website Cubs 1967 page.

The New Bill James Historical Baseball Abstract, Bill James, Free Press 2003.

The Hitless Wonders

Baseball Reference website 1906 Chicago White Sox statistics page.

Baseball Almanac website 1906 post-season page.

MLB.com website 1906 season re-cap.

The New Bill James Historical Baseball Abstract, Bill James, Free Press 2003.

The Image of Their Greatness, Honig and Ritter, Random House Value Publishing 1988.

Baseball Reference website 1906 Cincinnati Reds statistics page: http://www.baseball-reference. com/teams/CIN/1906.shtml.

Baseball Almanac website 1906 Reds page: http://www.baseball-almanac.com/teamstats/roster. php?y=1906&t=CIN.

Mob or No Mob

Eight Men Out, Eliot Asinof, Holt Paperback Edition 2001.

The Image of Their Greatness, Honig and Ritter, Random House Value Publishing 1988.

Chicago History Museum website article about Shoeless Joe Jackson and the 1919 White Sox.

Chicago White Sox website summary of 1919 White Sox season.

Baseball Reference website 1919 Chicago White Sox statistics page.

Baseball Almanac website 1919 White Sox page.

Answers.com website blurb on gambler and organized crime figure Arnold Rothstein.

Baseball Reference website 1919 Cincinnati Reds statistics page: http://www.baseball-reference.com/teams/CIN/1919.shtml.

Baseball Almanac website 1919 Reds page http://www.baseball-almanac.com/teamstats/roster.php?y=1919&t=CIN.

When Baseball Was Really Baseball

The Image of Their Greatness, Honig and Ritter, Random House Value Publishing 1988.

The New Bill James Historical Baseball Abstract, Bill James, Free Press 2003.

The Glory of Their Times, Laurence S. Ritter, Harper Perennial 2010 edition.

A DOZEN OTHER BOOKS OF STORIES ABOUT BASEBALL

Pages from Baseball's Past, by Craig P. Wright

Solid Fool's Gold: Detours on the Way to Conventional Wisdom, by Bill James

Fools Rush Inn: More Detours on the Way to Conventional Wisdom, by Bill James

Good Wood: The Story of the Baseball Bat, by Stuart Miller

Strat-O-Matic Fanatics: The Unlikely Success Story of a Game That Became an American Passion, by Glenn Guzzo

Walk Offs, Last Licks, and Final Outs: Baseball's Grand (and not-so-grand) Finales, by Bill Chuck and Jim Kaplan

The Lou Gehrig Story: Told by a Fan, by Sara Kaden Brunsvold

How Bill James Changed Our View of Baseball, edited by Gregory F. Augustine Pierce

Wild Cards: A Novel, by Ken Berris

Dear Frank: Babe Ruth, the Red Sox, and the Great War, by W. Nikola-Lisa

The Men Who Made the Yankees: The Odyssey of the World's Greatest Baseball Team from Baltimore to the Bronx, by W. Nikola-Lisa

Traded: Inside the Most Lopsided Trades in Baseball History, by Doug Decatur

Available from booksellers or call 800-397-2282
www.actasports.com